Bless the Imperfect

Bless the Imperfect

Meditations for Congregational Leaders

Kathleen Montgomery, Editor

Skinner House Books
Boston

www.skinnerhouse.org

Printed in the United States

Cover and text design by Suzanne Morgan
Photo of Kay Montgomery by Adrien Bisson

print ISBN: 978-1-55896-719-9
eBook ISBN: 978-1-55896-720-5

6 5 4 3 2 1
16 15 14 13

Library of Congress Cataloging-in-Publication Data

Bless the imperfect : meditations for congregational leaders / Kathleen Montgomery, editor.
    pages cm
  ISBN 978-1-55896-719-9 (pbk. : alk. paper)—ISBN 978-1-55896-720-5 (ebook)
 1. Leadership—Prayers and devotions. 2. Leadership—Religious aspects—Unitarian Universalist churches. I. Montgomery, Kathleen, editor of compilation.
  BV4597.53.L43M47 2013
  242'.69—dc23
                            2013023339

"The Paradox of Organized Religion" is adapted from an excerpt from *Governance and Ministry: Rethinking Board Leadership* by Dan Hotchkiss, © 2009 by The Alban Institute.

"The Rabbis" will be included in a book by Dan Hotchkiss on leadership in congregations, scheduled to be published by The Alban Institute in early 2015.

Dedicated to the last four UUA financial advisors. Their contributions have far outweighed the job description of that role and they've been central, though often invisible, to the health of the Association. I am deeply grateful to each of them.

Bob Lavender

Arnold Bradburd

Larry Ladd

Dan Brody

Contents

 **KATHLEEN (KAY) MONTGOMERY** was the first woman and first layperson to become executive vice president of the Unitarian Universalist Association. She held that role from 1985 until 2013, serving in the administrations of four UUA presidents. She is now retired, living in the Jamaica Plain neighborhood of Boston.

Preface

I've always thought that leadership was overrated. It's a skill, not a virtue. It's a skill that some people seem to develop as children and others learn through trial and error or by close observation, through mentors, or out of necessity. It's an important tool, one that makes change happen, but it isn't a virtue and leaders can—and do—do great good or great harm.

These meditations, written by some of the most thoughtful leaders in Unitarian Universalism, speak of leadership embedded in the values of our faith. They give some advice, acknowledge the problems, admit the imperfections. They exhort and challenge and tell amusing and lovely stories of both public and quiet leadership.

This collection is designed for those who choose to play a role in shaping the future of our congregations and our faith. Use it before a meeting or in private before a challenging moment. Use it to remind yourself of the need for humility and humor and courage in the course of your work toward justice and spiritual community.

—Kathleen Montgomery

Long-Haul People

Rudy Nemser

You find them in churches
when you're lucky;
other places too, though I mostly
only know ecclesiastical varieties.

Long-haul people,
upon whose shoulders
(and pocketbooks and casseroles
and daylight/nighttime hours)
a church is built and maintained
after the brass is tarnished and
cushions need re-stitching.

They pay their pledges full and on time
even when the music's modern;
support each canvass
though the sermons aren't always short;
mow lawns and come to suppers;
teach Sunday school when
there's no one else and they'll miss the service.

Asked what they think of the minister,
or plans for the kitchen renovation,
or the choral anthem, or Christmas pageant,

or color of the bathroom paint,
they'll reply: individuals and fashions
arrive and pass.
The church—their church—will be here, steady and hale.
For a long. Long time.
It will.
For long-haul people bless a church
with a very special blessing.

Just Regular Folks

Jane Ranney Rzepka

In the 1930s, of course, times were tough. During that period, members of our church were accustomed to pledging either twenty-five cents a week, fifty cents, or one dollar a week. In the 1929–30 church year, all the church members fulfilled their pledges of thirteen dollars for the year, or twenty-six dollars, or fifty-two.

But as the Depression continued, our ledger books begin to show tiny numbers at the bottom of each page. Five cents. Two dollars. Twelve dollars. And then a little "s." Five cents "short" of the pledge. Twelve dollars short. Just what one would expect during the Depression.

But picture this: Picture more numbers appearing at the bottom of the ledger. Four dollars. Eighty cents. Seven dollars. Thirty cents. And after these numbers, the tiny letter "o." Four dollars "over" the pledge. Eighty cents over.

There is no evidence in our records of a special appeal from the Board of Trustees, no traces of public discussion, only the quiet generosity of the people. For every pledge that had to fall short, one of many generous people overpaid to compensate.

The history of our churches tells us Gandhi was never a member. Mother Teresa never belonged either. King Midas never showed up, nor Bill Gates, for that matter. Just regular folks, like us. They dedicated their babies, they worshipped, they reached out to do their part in the world, they tended one another, they kept the place going, they tried to live their best lives.

In those old days, Samuel Eliot, a big shot from the Unitarian headquarters, stood outside our church to dedicate a new building, and he said, "My friends, let us not forget that the church of the spirit must be forever building. You are linking your personal religion to the spiritual life of this whole community, and in this high endeavor, I bid you Godspeed."

Song for the Unsung

Steve J. Crump

You make the coffee, set up the tables, and organize the cleaning
  when the rest of us have gone home.

You know where the brooms and the supplies are kept.
You run to the store in the nick of time.
You find the great stuff to sell at the fundraiser.

You remember to use "I" language.
You speak passionately with a clear voice and listen with open-
  mindedness.
You consider your tone when you speak.
You say you want to be part of the solution, part of the healing,
  by hanging in there.

You come up with new ideas.
You gracefully accept the group choosing someone else's idea.
You step up to make the extra contribution.
You make welcoming room for others.
You acknowledge children and are happy to be around them.

You hold a child, hold a confidence, and hold a hand.
You go the extra mile, contribute the extra dollar, and give the
  benefit of doubt.
You know that church life is all about relationships.

And because you know this, your spiritual discipline of forgiveness
is always at hand.

You, with your presence alone, offer a holy companionship.
You accompany others in their dark night of the soul.

You do what you do because you can.
You often wish you could do more.
You labor not for praise or for a song but for the good in the doing
of work.

But we sing this song of praise for you—the unsung in our
church.
And our hearts are glad in the singing because we know the many
things you do.
We appreciate you very much.

Hansel and Gretel

Lynn Ungar

"Read it again!" she says,
and again we do. The same
disaster predictably re-enacted,
night to night. "Don't go in!"
I want to warn them, "It's a trap!"
But children rarely listen, and
storybook characters, never.
When they see that candy-covered cottage
their entrance is inevitable,
like the mosquito bite you swear
you will not scratch and always do,
and always make it worse.

Each decision is invariably
a rigged game. The witch
is always ravenous and grasping,
the children neglected and naïve.
Preach all you like about conversion,
about goodness and unending grace—
you know the witch will never
lose her taste for the sweet
resilient flesh of boys.

Night after night we stumble
into the forest of our fears,
and night after night we're duly caught.
Every morning we awake
to the same reports of mayhem and
every morning we poke forward
some narrow stick of ourselves,
hoping to get by uneaten
one more day.

But listen. Each time through
the story we can drop
a small white stone. Others
have too—I've seen them
glowing in the moonlight,
a nightly shifting of the scene,
building a path both ragged and new.
Next time, look down. Tear your vision
from the gingerbread house.
Drop a stone.
Tell the children.

Dragon Lady at the Chalice!

Vanessa Rush Southern

I started my current ministry in August of 2001. The community I serve is a commuter suburb of New York City and I started just a month before the twin towers and our sense of security both came crashing down. On Tuesday the 11th we met people at the trains in shock and covered in dust. On Sunday I preached my first sermon to them.

It is hard enough, under normal circumstances, to know how to launch a new ministry, how to take risks and build trust and create a sense of new possibilities. It felt almost impossible in the days leading up to that first Sunday to know how to do that. In addition to everything else, we were also reconstructing our building and so meeting in a middle school gym. Most Sundays that year I preached under a basketball hoop, artificial lights buzzing, with the congregation seated awkwardly in bleachers. The deck was stacked against us.

That first Sunday, I chiseled every word I wrote with painstaking care. Nothing was haphazard. When I showed up, the gym was packed. Like everywhere else in the country, people gathered whenever and however they could for solace, and also this group just wanted to see their new minister.

Silence. Music. Worship began. I rose and spoke of our gathering, struck the match to light our chalice, but shuddered mid-gesture. Because, you see, no sooner had I struck the match, then I felt a searing pain in the tender mucous membranes of the inside of my nose. I held my breath instinctively, realizing in that moment that for the first time in my career—and never since—I had inhaled whatever magical chemical it is with which they coat the end of matches. And, in case you are wondering, it hurts.

Trying not to show my panic, holding back the tears in my eyes, I waited for the pain to subside before I lit the chalice. With the scary episode over, I released my held breath. This was when *smoke came out of my nose*! It came out in a neat stream, the way a snorting dragon looks in fairy tales.

Dragon Lady in the chancel, ladies and gentlemen, I wanted to yell out. And thus begins our ministry together!

No one has ever said that they saw the smoke coming from my nose that day. However, in the moment, as I stood there, appalled at how my first day on the job—my first real day—was going, I did let go of a whole lot of expectations. It was clear I wasn't going to be flawless, graceful, or safe in this job, no more or less than I had been any of those things ever before in my life. I was going to be me. Stumbling, awkward and slipping on banana peels along with the best of them.

Truth be told, most spiritual wisdom says that is enough. Imperfection leaves plenty of room for remarkable wisdom and courage. And twelve years down the road, I can say that this congregation and I have done great ministry together. And we have done it all despite and amidst their flaws and mine.

I try to remind myself regularly that Moses had a stutter. Jesus could lose his temper. Mother Theresa doubted her faith for most of her career. We do the best we can, you and I. We do the best we can on our own and together. And, all fire-breathing and tough circumstances aside, it is amazing how astoundingly well we manage to do! It is a good thing to remember when we have a bad day or week or are cursing the less polished parts of ourselves.

Bless the imperfect leaders. Bless the astounding beauty they usher into the world. Bless us all.

How to Be a UU Leader

Denise Taft Davidoff

1. Breathe deeply.
2. Relinquish control.
3. Learn to pray.
4. Play fair.
5. Temper narcissism.
6. Read poetry.
7. Internalize patience.
8. Listen intently.
9. Admit errors.
10. Breathe deeply.

A Sweet Mystery

Sarah Lammert

One morning, Manhattan awoke early to discover a sweet, intoxicating smell wafting over city stoops and park benches, high rises and subway entrances. It was as if a giant pancake were floating in the air above the island, dripping a fine mist of maple syrup.

Had it not been 2005 and the wounds of 9/11 still so fresh, the citizens of that great city might have gone about their days with a smile playing on their lips, dreaming of childhood breakfasts and craving doughnuts and baklava. But people were scared by the odors, and the 311 emergency line buzzed and buzzed. Men and women in hazard suits were dispatched with air canisters to capture the suspicious scent, but by the time they arrived the smell was gone just as suddenly as it had arrived.

It would be four years and several more maple syrup incidents before determined city officials traced the odor to a factory using fenugreek, a harmless clover-like seed, to produce food flavors. Finally the mystery of the bit-o-honey fragrance was solved, and the people of Manhattan could step out confidently, assured that someone wasn't taunting them periodically with clouds of sweet but potentially toxic perfume.

What does this have to do with leading congregational change? We live in an age of anxiety brought on by an unpredictable and even violent rate of change in our society. In the past, certain issues may have been managed through quiet, top-down shifts in congregational life. Today, this kind of approach can easily provoke and confuse congregants. People don't like surprises in congregations or in communities, even if they are wrapped in sweetness. Instead, the ministerial or lay leader of today is well advised to follow the practice of the airline industry. Airlines have discovered that their customers will bear unexpected interruptions of their travel plans with a fair amount of stoicism and grace as long as they are informed at appropriate intervals about what is going on. Informing people—and even more, inviting input during periods of change—allows them to keep up with their leaders, who might otherwise charge ahead, forgetting to look over their shoulder to see whether anyone is following.

Leading change requires vision; but even more it requires transparency to engage the imagination and support of the community. Don't let the aromatic seeds of transformation be mistaken for a terrorist takeover of your beloved community. Instead, nurture clarity and confidence so that you can all breathe deep, take heart, and stay the course of change.

Charge to the Parish Minister

Laurel Hallman

Nourish our spiritual lives
    with your preaching and teaching,
    and by your presence among us.

Help us to celebrate our joys and grieve our losses
    so that we will know we are not
    alone in life's journey.

Help us remember
    the greater glory to which
    all our labors are directed.

Connect us
    with the great teachings, poetry, and rituals
    of humanity so that we might apply the wisdom
    of the ages to our lives and times.

Help us to envision
    future possibilities,
    even as we encounter our
    human and institutional limitations.

Help us focus our actions
    that we not dissipate our energies

in that which is irrelevant
to our unique calling.

Encourage and advise us
as we seek to create community
in these days of social isolation.

Help us define
the boundaries and requirements of
membership in our church,
as well as remain open to the gifts
that new members bring.

Help us not to take ourselves too seriously.
Give us a good word when we need it.

Help us ensure
that qualified leadership will follow us
in the years to come.

Challenge us
to confront the insidious forces of evil
both within and without.

Help us to conduct
the business of this church
in an ethical, humane, and effective manner.

Help connect us
with the larger denomination.

Help us to focus
our service to humanity so that

we might leave this world a better place
than we found it.

Serve as an ambassador
     from our church
     to the larger community.

Help us to be responsible stewards of
     the religious artifacts given to us
     by our forebears in faith.

     the religious tradition handed down
     through the centuries by
     Unitarians and Universalists

     the purposes and principles upheld
     by the members of our church since
     its inception

     the memories, stories, and
     lives of people who have created
     our church.

Messy and Imperfect Beloved Community

Laila Ibrahim

I have been going to the same church for a very long time. For nearly thirty years most Sundays I have walked through our beautiful redwood doors. In all those years I have filled a variety of leadership positions, from OWL teacher to Board president, usher coordinator to stewardship co-chair. And in all those years my congregation has had ample opportunity to disappoint me.

I am disappointed when people don't think my justice project is the one we should collectively work on; I am disappointed when people want different music than I do; I am disappointed that we don't all agree that our Children's Ministry is the most important priority in the church; I am disappointed that people don't give enough time, talent, or treasure to the church as I do. I am disappointed . . . well, you get the idea. In nearly thirty of years of relationship, there have been lots of disappointments.

Two or three times over the years, I have been so disappointed that I seriously questioned remaining in my congregation. I have wondered if church is actually real. I have doubted its ability to provide the salvation of which we speak: lived beloved community. On those occasions I have thought, Fuck it. I can just stop going to church for awhile or . . . forever. But staying away has never helped me through such times. Rather, coming in closer, telling people about my spiritual crisis—listening, sharing, caring, and worshipping

—have helped me know that this is where I belong, even when church is the source of my frustration and disappointment.

Because we are not in church to be with people who want to sing the same music, or rally for same cause, or attend the same retreats. We are in church to learn to love better. And learning to love better can only happen when we love past our disappointments and return to a place of acceptance and affirmation. This is true in our personal lives, in our work lives, and in our church lives. It is a deep spiritual practice.

At my best, as a religious person, as a Unitarian Universalist, as a member of this First Unitarian Church of Oakland, I am called to love whoever else walks through these doors. I don't need to like everyone. Not everyone is who I would choose for a friend. Not everyone agrees about what we are here to do. But if I am living up to my best values, I offer care and respect and commitment to each member, friend, and guest of my beloved community.

In the end, we can all try our best to live out our faith as Unitarian Universalists—through study, conversation, service, and commitment. We forgive ourselves and forgive others as we stumble through. We disagree, we annoy, we flake out on one another. And we worship, we support, we hold, and we affirm one another.

There is really only one choice: between imperfect community and no community. Again and again, we are all called to choose to commit ourselves to building a more just, more diverse, and yet ever messy and imperfect beloved community.

Start Right Here

Gary E. Smith

I believe we have a home, we have a spiritual tent, we have sacred spaces that are large enough to hold those who hunger for something more in this lifetime. I believe that we have a message that speaks to the deepest places of the human spirit as it cries out in its hunger and thirst. I believe that Unitarian Universalism and places like your congregation and mine are places where dreams have become realities for people, where they have been fed, where they have been given living waters.

I believe we as Unitarian Universalists have for too long made our own happy little communities and have been terrified to keep the doors open and let new people in, afraid to grow because God knows what will change, and surprise, surprise, we have stayed the tiny little religious movement we have deserved to be.

I believe we can become a force to be reckoned with if only we will find our voice and our witness and our courage and our leadership and our message and our commitment. I believe only our pettiness and our silly fights about this or that will do us in. I believe we can stay small if we choose. We can offer horrible sermons, a thin liturgy, a cold shoulder to visitors. We can push our children out of the way. We can throw a buck a week into the offering plate. We can sing only the hymns that have words with which every last person in the sanctuary can agree. We can revise our bylaws every six weeks. We can let the other religious communities in town help to feed the hungry, clothe the naked, and visit the imprisoned. And we can stay small.

Something can start right here with you and me. We can claim our leadership. We can name it and claim it. We can build trust in the places we call home. We can be Somebody in this movement and mentor those congregations just a little smaller than we are to grow and to surpass us. We can be selfless and non-territorial. We can let somebody else claim the credit. We can keep our eye on the vision.

This is what I believe.

Losers

John Corrado

In a culture that worships winners,
some people say the church is a place for losers
—and they are right!
This *is* a place for losers.

This is a place for people who have
lost their hair,
lost their teeth,
lost their place,
lost their memories,
lost their savings,
lost their jobs.

It's a place for people who have
lost their parents,
lost the love of their life, and even
lost their children.

It's a place for people who have
lost their way,
lost their faith, and, worst of all,
lost all hope.

The church is a place for losers—us!

Let's see who we are,
and how we are,
and how much we need and can help one another.

We are the losers.
God bless us everyone!

Something Left Over

John Buehrens

John Ertha had been raised in one of the two African-American families in Bangor, Maine. A poet and skeptic, he'd become a Unitarian and had married, across racial lines, a Universalist. I was first introduced to him by another African-American UU, Bill Sinkford, a college roommate — later my successor as president of our denomination; then the president of its national youth organization, Liberal Religious Youth. Bill had been a counselor at the summer camp for youth leadership development that John Ertha started. It was called Homestead. It had a simple philosophy: Each and every one of us is capable of being a leader. "Leadership," taught Ertha, "is simply having something left over, after taking care of yourself, to care for someone or something else." Children could be leaders. Campers led some workshops, even though they were younger than most counselors. They came to a lakeside camp in Maine from urban ghettos and suburban UU congregations. Some paid to be there; some were neither paid nor paying, just learning; others were paid a bit. Everyone grew.

Shy, bookish, I would not have become any sort of leader, much less a religious leader devoted to human rights in all its forms, were it not for what I learned at Homestead. It was there that I first grew a beard, at twenty-one, to play the part of Tevye, in *Fiddler on the Roof*! Musical theater taught me. I had never acted, or sung in public. My young director, son of a black jazz musician and a Jewish actress, was all of fourteen—doing his tenth production. "Tradition! Tradition! Without it, we would be like, like . . . a fiddler on the roof!" So privileged white liberal kids learned, alongside ghetto kids, values preserved by another oppressed people, who had survived pogroms.

Every morning there was a theme talk, attended by six-year-olds and adults alike. Every evening there was worship. Once each three-week camp session there was an election for various leadership roles: everyone voting, from the oldest to the youngest; no heads down on desks to avoid seeing who voted against you. There were open speeches about your virtues and failings, with the promise of what Ertha called "a respectable re-entry" if—like me one time— you were voted out of office as a leader who had failed to listen adequately to the followers. The Sunday-night worship after elections was typically an Ertha-crafted "ante-bellum service." It began:

"Let us return now, sisters and brothers, to that lost Eden of non-verbal, bio-psychic functioning, both in the ontogenic and the phylogenic senses . . . and then speak some words of comfort to our brethren in distress." Then, black and white together, we'd sing spirituals like "Steal Away, Steal Away Home, I Ain't Got Long to Stay Here."

Ertha would recite, from memory, Paul Laurence Dunbar's "Ante-Bellum Sermon," and others of us, playing deacon, would add readings from James Weldon Johnson's "God's Trombones." This early experience of inter-racial worship is still deeply inscribed on my soul. It's my lived version of what I heard, when I was sixteen, in Dr. King's words: "I have a dream."

Call it "something left over." It's what makes leaders learn both how to stay resilient, and how to most effectively challenge and inspire future leaders.

The Church That Doesn't Matter

Kelly Weisman Asprooth-Jackson

In the church that doesn't matter, there are no quarrels, no arguments, and no one ever says anything they regret at the meeting to discuss the sanctuary's new paint color. There is nothing to inspire such passionate intensity because none of the decisions of the church touch anyone's heart, and no one lives or dies by its choices, or even feels for a moment like they might. Everything is easy as pie.

In the church that doesn't matter, no one has to ask for money, or even talk about it much; there is always enough to go around. There is always enough because no matter how much there is, there is always less to do with it than that. The vision always shrinks to under-match the means. So canvass season is always a breeze.

In the church that doesn't matter, no one ever disagrees with the preacher's sermon. The music is always just fine. There is never a fight about the liturgy, not even if they do joys and sorrows (and not even if they stop doing joys and sorrows). There is never any controversy because no one ever says anything they really care about, and no one else ever seems to care. And so, the service is always equally inoffensive at both nine o'clock and eleven.

The sounds of children during worship, the recruitment of Sunday School teachers, the compensation of professional religious educators and the size and condition of space for religious education—none of these things are ever talked about or thought about in the church that doesn't matter. Those issues just take care of themselves somehow.

No one ever has to clean up in the church that doesn't matter. Or figure out the old electrical system, or consult the building codes, or climb a ladder. If no one bothers to make coffee on Sunday, no one complains, and if no one greets the visitors, no one seems to mind. Everything is easier in the church that doesn't matter.

The total solution to all the frustrations of congregational life requires no consultants, manuals, or webinars. Simply avoid, at all costs, meaning and purpose and anything that might lead you to either or both. Whatever you do, do not let yourself care about the people around you, or the covenant you share.

Yet, knowing this, we still decide again and again to ask tough questions, take real risks, do work that needs doing, and tell the truth. We get out of bed on Sunday morning, answer that email, make something for the bake sale and give our time and attention to a meeting every third Thursday. We ask each other how we're doing, and mean it. We make phone calls and craft projects for the first-grade class—we offer our gifts, both humble and great. And we do these things, sometimes in joy, and sometimes not in joy, because they are done in service of a church that matters.

Theology of Inclusion

Janice Marie Johnson

Masakhane, my theology of inclusion, is a rich and resonant word from the Nguni family of languages of South Africa, of which Zulu and Xhosa are two. Loosely translated into English it means, "Let us build together."

Building a multicultural sensibility is difficult, transformative work as well as a much-needed leadership skill that allows us to plug into our Power Source as we embrace joy, solemnity, reverence, and faith. It requires us to bolster our spiritual strength and deepen our resilience. A theology of inclusion is a divinely inspired, intentional reaching out to "the other." It invites us to disregard resistance, love beyond belief, and honor inclusion. We provide the hands and feet, knowing that God provides the ability to do the impossible, to make a way out of no way.

Whether we know someone or not, we are called to love greatly. bell hooks urges and advises educators-in-training to love their students even before they know them. That is another way of describing the theology of inclusion: extending the circle to all knowing that each of us stands on holy ground.

> He drew a circle that shut me out—
> Heretic, rebel, a thing to flout.
> But Love and I had the wit to win:
> We drew a circle that took him in!

With these simple words, Edwin Markham's "Outwitted" offers a perfect example of the theology of inclusion. If we equate love with God—as I believe Markham intended—then we understand our relationship to the divine as a partnership, one in which the divine provides us with the power of intention, and we provide the "person-power."

We would do well to follow the Haudenosaunee (aka Iroquois) example of planning now—not just for our children, or their children—but for the seventh generation. The theology of inclusion calls us to ensure that our children and all future generations have the right to grow up in a world free of "the isms." I believe that a force greater than ourselves tells us that we need to act. We know, instinctively, how to be of help to others, but we are good at resisting our instincts, especially when they tell us to do something that takes us out of our comfort zone.

We are often called to do the difficult, if not the seemingly impossible, and it is vital to our spiritual growth that we not ignore these challenges. If you're human, you hear the call. But hearing and responding are two different things.

May we ever respond to the call of leadership.

May we ever give thanks in the great spirit of "Masakhane."

The Power of Truth

Mark Belletini

After working with both synagogue and church leaders who always made excuses for why things couldn't move forward, Rabbi Edwin Friedman offered this particularly fine comment: "I therefore stopped listening to the content of everyone's complaints, and, irrespective of the location of their problem, or the nature of their institution, began saying the exact same thing to everyone: 'You have to get up before your people and give an *I Have a Dream* speech.'"

Lest you claim that Friedman is setting the bar too high for anyone without King's remarkable oratorical skills, let me offer an interpretation of his meaning by telling you the story of Marge.

Marge and her husband Bill were long-time members of the second congregation I was fortunate to serve. Marge was articulate, thoughtful, and smart, and never missed a service unless she was away, which was rare. She shared her forthright skepticism about some of the ideas about worship I brought to the table ("You're not going to read from the Bible, are you?") but never tried to get me to change my style. I always felt warm toward her because I rather favor direct, engaged people who don't complain so much as plainly state their own view.

Marge was not one to run for office, although she did end up sitting on the Board once. She was not an orator, spoke only for herself, and often had a reserved presence.

But this does not mean she was not a most excellent leader.

When Jean, a student from Starr King School, applied to serve as an intern at the church, the Board hesitated. Jean was in a wheelchair. Our simple homespun buildings were *mostly* accessible. But this student, an excellent leader herself, simply suggested that in order for the buildings to be *totally* accessible, the door of one of the bathrooms had to be re-hung to open in the other direction, and a very small ramp had to be built to let her chair negotiate the single step into the church office.

"We don't have that money in our budget," opined one Board member. "I don't know if we can deal with that," worried another. "And anyway, who has the ability around here to design and build such a ramp?"

But Marge simply said, "It seems to me that if we mean what we say when we espouse our Unitarian Universalist principles of justice and equal access, then the simple solutions Jean just suggested *might best have been accomplished twenty years ago.* I think the ramp and the door need to be in place by Friday at the latest."

And they were.

And Jean interned with us most excellently.

Note, Marge didn't hammer a single nail, design the ramp, or even organize the work party. She just spoke the truth, and let the truth do its work, addressing both our stated commitments and our *dream* for our future as a congregation.

Leadership often requires patience. And stamina, certainly. But the urgency of the dream was part of the truth Marge expressed at that Board meeting, and I am convinced she was right.

Telling the truth, and attaching that truth to the religious principles by which *we say* we live our lives, is quite simply, a spiritual act. For leadership, according to an elegant poem by religious educator Kimberly Beyer Nelson, is the way "we cup our hands" to "hold the peace" we *say* we affirm, "even when the sirens begin . . . and words . . . rend."

But whether urgent or played out over a long time, whether expressed by one voice or many, good leadership is the sure tinder that kindles the chalice flame, and illustrates the dream of *any* congregation which desires to illumine the world: both beyond—and within—its open doors.

A *Prayer for Leaders*

William F. Schulz

O God.

I am a leader. O God!

Teach me to practice patience and forbearance in the wake of every comment, no matter how inane.

Sustain me in the face of hidden motives, manipulation, passive aggressiveness, and aggressive passivity.

Grace me with the knowledge that progress is halting and resistance is to be expected.

Make me a person of integrity and align our collective vision with our organizational health.

Remind me regularly of our long-term mission and larger faith.

Help me to worry less about my legacy and more about whether I make glad the paths of those who journey with me.

Insist that I laugh.

Let me never forget that "this too will pass."

Grace me with gratitude.

I am a leader. O God!

Amen.

The Paradox of Organized Religion

Dan Hotchkiss

Religion at its best is no friend of the status quo. Religion transforms people; no one touches holy ground and stays the same. Religious leaders stir the pot by pointing to the contrast between life as it is and life as it should be, and urging us to close the gap. Religious insights provide the handhold that people need to criticize injustice, rise above self-interest, and take risks to provide healing to a wounded world.

Organization, on the other hand, conserves. Institutions capture, schematize, and codify persistent patterns of activity. People sometimes say, "Institutions are conservative," and smile as if they had said something clever. But conservation is what institutions do. A well-ordered congregation lays down schedules, puts policies on paper, places people in positions, and generally brings order out of chaos. Organizations can be flexible, creative, and iconoclastic, but only by resisting some of their most basic instincts.

No wonder "organized religion" is so difficult! Congregations create sanctuaries where people can nurture and inspire each other—with results no one can predict. The stability of a religious institution is necessary for the instability that religious transformation brings. The need to balance both sides of this paradox— the transforming power of religion and the stabilizing power of organization—makes leading congregations a unique challenge.

Let the Wrong Ones In

Susan Ritchie

We often speak of the mantle of leadership as involving an inheritance from the past. We sing that "what they dreamed be ours to do," and speak of torches given to our temporary care as they travel from the past to the future. Yet in a progressive religious tradition, this is especially challenging. Most of our personal identities and theologies would shock our religious ancestors. They did not dream us, unless in their worst nightmare. So who did? What legacy can be honestly invoked to sound an authentic note for progressive leadership?

Somewhere along the line someone left this tradition open for me. Someone invited me in, someone made the way for me even though there is no equivalent for me in our forebears' imagination. And when things have been bad, when I have been bad, this tradition has carried me around in my sorry little basket and given me over and over again the invitation to relationship, the invitation to be human, as human as I dare. When I am privileged to lead, I feel the power of this invitation behind me. But who issued it?

In the early days of American congregationalism, membership in the church was tightly controlled. The covenant of membership was restricted to the saints: those who were destined for heaven and who could prove it before a parsimonious clergy and a small number of pious church members. But many of the people in the pews refused this narrow view. When the minister preached about how the covenant—the very love of God and the love of the people—was reserved for the elect, the people heard something different. They heard the offer of covenant extended to all who desired its embrace. Eventually, this generosity led to a different church: a church with doors held open wide, our church.

And it is this spirit that I imagine speaking to our leaders, saying:

Remind us of how for all but five minutes of our history we have been the wrong people. Help us to identify, name, and invite all the wrong people who may, in fact, turn out to be right. Show us those who need our invitation to participate in a whole and holy humanity. May your leadership be one of radical hospitality and inclusion.

What Is Your Ministry?

Bruce T. Marshall

Leadership in a Unitarian Universalist congregation involves ministry. Not just those who are ordained; everybody has a ministry. What is yours?

Maurice Sendak, author of *Where the Wild Things Are*, once observed, "There must be more to life than having everything." That is, there must be more to life than the endless pursuit of "everything." Ministry involves witnessing to that something more, offering service or testimony, standing in awe or taking a stand, or engaging in a mission that affirms, yes, there is more to life.

All ministries are not the same. In Paul's *Letter to the Romans*, he observes, "We have different gifts, based on the grace that was given to us." We are given different talents and so there are many ways of having a ministry.

Evangelical Christians are good at recognizing this. They're good at extending the concept of ministry to all. It's one reason that evangelical Christian churches can be so vital.

A church consultant told of working with a super-mega congregation, something like 10,000 members and growing. He described wandering through the building late one night and coming upon a group of custodians taking a break. He complimented them on the condition of the facilities. One of the custodians replied, "We are all ministers. When we're cleaning a room at night, we think about what's going to happen there during the day and how we can serve that aim." They weren't just doing a job; they were offering service.

What is your ministry? How do you respond to that call of something more? Perhaps there's a mission you need to fulfill. Or a message to learn and convey. Or a truth you must witness to, or a value you are called to affirm. Perhaps there's a journey you need to undertake. Or a vision you must seek and explore. Maybe your ministry involves being present for another person: someone for whom you can make a difference.

As leaders, part of our own ministries involves enabling others to find theirs. We ask not just, "What is my ministry?" but also "What is yours?" And "How can we help each other in the ministries we share?" Strength and spirit grow in a congregation whose members participate in ministry.

"I don't know what your destiny will be," Albert Schweitzer said, "but one thing I know: the only ones among you who will be really happy are those who will have sought and found how to serve."

Ask Someone Else

Peter Morales

The biblical story of Jonah begins when Jonah hears a call from God telling him to go at once to Nineveh. So what does he do? He immediately heads out at full speed in the *opposite* direction and tries to hide in a place where God won't find him.

Resistance to follow God's call is a common theme in the Hebrew scriptures. After Moses sees the burning bush on Mount Horeb and hears God tell him that he has been chosen to return to Egypt and free God's people, Moses raises all kinds of objections: They won't believe me. I am not eloquent. I am slow of tongue. Finally, he comes right out and begs God to send someone else.

It's easy to say, as Moses did: Please ask someone else. When we are asked to take on a big responsibility, we may feel Jonah's urge to run as far away as possible.

How many times have you ducked a new challenge? How many times have you wanted to? How many times have all of us unwittingly undermined those who have had the courage and commitment to lead? How many times have we criticized when we should have been silent? How many times have we neglected to thank our leaders? How often have we failed to ask what we could do to help?

Everything good that happens when people act together happens because somebody said yes to taking on a big responsibility.

When I was young I held some mistaken notions about leadership—notions which I share with lots of people. I thought of leaders as charismatic, eloquent, dynamic, tireless, fearless, and decisive. I thought of them as somehow larger than life. I came to see that my images of leaders were silly fantasies. Leaders come in a variety of styles. Some of the very best are soft spoken and self-effacing.

Research shows that four qualities of leaders stand out. Leaders whom people admire are honest, forward looking, competent, and have an enthusiasm that inspires. More than anything, leaders are credible. Leadership is a relationship based on mutual trust. Trust empowers the leader and the leader empowers others.

Are you honest? Are you forward looking? In what areas are you competent? Are you enthusiastic about the things you care about deeply? Do people trust you? If so, you are a leader, even if you don't realize it.

But the real questions are not about whether you are a leader. The real questions are: What do you care about passionately? Where can you make a difference?

Don't resist what is calling to you in the depths of your being. The world needs your gifts. Desperately. No one else can do what you can. No one. Lead on. Lead on.

Prayer for the Stubborn

Vanessa Rush Southern

O name for that which holds us and will not let us go,
O force of vision in our lives,
Source of dreams that hold us captive and give us reasons to
    wake:
Help us to find the strength to persist.

When despair comes knocking, or the road seems too dry and
    dusty,
When circumstance conspires against greatness or the honest tell-
    ing of truths,
Help us to find the power and inspiration to endure.

Or, at the very least, help us find our way back to the simple
    rituals of love and justice that can resuscitate our dreams.

In this life, may we
Love deeply
Act in humble, but determined ways
And never waver.

May we persist until the sun sets
And wake again to persist once more

Until the world of our boldest aspirations is made real by passion,
And also by endurance, stubborn faithfulness, and persistence:
The trademarks and engine of a noble and visionary life.

For the sake of all we cherish, O God,
Keep us stubborn.

The Unseen Spiritual Discipline of Administration

Sue Phillips

Upon answering the call to elected leadership, most people do not usually expect to talk with bookkeepers, get bids for roof repairs, or negotiate differences of opinion about carpet colors. And a call to ministry generally does not include dreams of supervising staff, copying orders of service, or calling plumbers.

But Spirit works in mysterious ways, and as it turns out the "unseen spiritual discipline of administration," as described by Rev. Victoria Safford, is the earthly substance of much congregational leadership. Much of what religious leaders do is unseen, because it happens outside of Sunday mornings, beyond the sight of most congregants. Even more to the point, we tend to underappreciate "administration" as a ministry because its aims appear so thoroughly secular. On the flip side, lay leaders can feel mired in everyday church management issues, and sometimes wonder how their church work began to feel so much like . . . work. Church administration without Spirit is indeed just work by another name.

This is where Safford's insightful observation hints at the many spiritual dimensions of congregational leadership. Meaning is being negotiated every time people come together for a common purpose. Values are always being prioritized and practiced. The soulful question at the heart of congregational leadership—

the essence that makes it different from secular pursuits—is: What meaning will we make, and which values will we serve?

Church administration is genuine religious leadership when that meaning and those values take a prominent place, along with Spirit, at staff and Board meetings. The simplest spiritual practices —prayer, *lectio divina*, singing, sharing testimonials, silence—can alchemize everyday acts of administration into holy practice.

But the secular substance of management and administration can only be transformed through *practice*, which is why spiritual discipline is required. Depth doesn't descend on church staff meetings just because someone reads opening words. Deeper meaning emerges when people actively practice going deep together. Every moment a Board or committee shares spiritual practice, however modest, and every time they cast their work in terms of meaning-making and values-living, is a holy moment. Administration, which is *everyday life in institutional form*, is redeemed from meaninglessness by this sacred effort.

What We Love, We Empower

Patrick T. O'Neill

What we love, we empower. We can't claim to love justice as long as we are willing to tolerate oppression or racism. We can't claim to love peace, unless somehow, in some way, we are seeking to make peace a reality in the world and in our personal lives.

We work for what we love. We invest in what we love. We try to become worthy of what we love and of the people we love. We give of our time, our energies, our attention and our resources so that what we love might thrive.

This principle applies to our church as well. Becoming a member is also about empowerment, though we don't always think of it that way. By joining a church, we declare that what the church stands for, the principles it teaches, the works it engages, the community it strives to become are all things we hold close to our hearts. By being members, we commit to empower this little institution.

And we have a right to expect that this church will empower us in return. It will call us to higher ground, to greater love, greater compassion, greater caring for the world and its troubles, for those suffering and their pains, for the deprived and their needs. It will empower us by calling us to live out our ideals and our principles in everyday life, in everyday relationships. It will empower our children too, if we have them. It will teach them tolerance and respect for the good and the holy. It will teach them self-love and love for others. It will provide safety and encouragement and community in times of celebration and of loss.

This is our great covenant and compact as members of the church. This is what we are here to do and to be for one another. By what we do here, by what we contribute each in our own way here, by the people we become here, by the ideals and the visions that we embrace and follow, by the families that we help to shape here in this church—we increase the store of love and justice in this world.

The Exceptional Moment of Our Unique Faith

Doug Zelinski

If the crux of Unitarian Universalism were reduced to a few points in space and time, they would be those potent moments just before and just after we keep a promise, or break it. All that is exceptional about being human and becoming whole is crystalized in these decisive microseconds:

~ Will I say "hello" to the visitor standing awkwardly near the sanctuary door or not?

~ Do I stay connected to Miguel even though he just voted against my idea?

~ Do I acknowledge the tug on my heart and wallet that asks me to really wrestle with the amount of my pledge?

~ Will I or will I not risk feeling unsure and uninformed as I step outside my comfort zone and spend time with those of other races, classes or generations on their terms rather than mine?

~ Will I expose my need for wholeness, my hope for forgiveness, my longing to belong, and my desire to matter?

People in all faith communities face microseconds like these. Sometimes we "live into" these moments and consciously wrestle with our instinct to fight, flee or freeze. Rising above these instincts to respond rather than react makes us human and moves us toward wholeness. That this power to become whole is so concentrated in these common moments is what makes them extraordinary.

Sometimes we subconsciously squelch these moments by automatically retreating into the ideology of our particular belief or non-belief. We may then spend time feeling wounded or righteous, debating, competing or even warring over religion.

Unique among the faiths, Unitarian Universalism proclaims the ordinary but decisive moments of human agency as the key to creating beloved community rather than a particular system of belief. We ask: How do we strive for communities of wholeness, with ourselves and with creation? What must we promise to make this so? How do we "begin again" after we break our promises? These are the questions of covenant. We are not exceptional in our perfection of covenanted community, but we are called to be exceptional in our promotion of it.

And this is why we must shed the current (and sometimes justified) fear of "exceptionalism" as vain individualism. With humility, let us realize that since ours is a "faith beyond belief," we are the stewards of a great gift desperately needed in this day and age.

To share this gift we need to extend ourselves further into new and different kinds of communities, bringing the message of covenant. And to share this message with humility, we must remember how difficult it can be to rise above our instincts during the extraordinary microseconds of living in covenant and to marvel at the Grace that makes it possible.

Nothing Is Static

Manish Mishra-Marzetti

The ground shifts, sometimes slowly,
sometimes like an earthquake,
reminding us that the solidity
we often love and seek
is an illusion.

The crumbling dust of the desert plains,
the moist fertility of farmlands,
the eroding coastline of tidal shores,
all are changing.

Committees dissolve or are created,
leaders retire or step away,
ministers come and go,
by-laws are amended.

New experiences,
lead to new truths,
which foster
evolution;

the natural course of life
always pushing us
toward greater understandings

of what it means
to be human.

Everything about our existence
points toward change,
flexibility, and
dynamic re-creation.

And it's hard because
change involves loss.

Can we hold the losses well,
while not holding ourselves back?

The ground shifts, sometimes slowly,
sometimes like an earthquake;
nothing is static.

Stepping Back, Moving Forward

Robert McKetchnie

One day when I was twelve years old my father announced that we needed a driveway along the side of our house. I remember thinking, "Good idea—there will be that much less lawn for me to mow!" A few days later an earthmover arrived and cut a very large rectangle into the lawn between my house and my neighbor's. The rectangle was wide enough for two cars to pass each other easily and it ran about one hundred feet up from the street.

When the earthmover was done, a dump truck appeared and left a pile of sand in the middle of the rectangle that reached about half as high as our three-story house. As soon as the truck left, I made my way to the top of the pile. My elderly next-door neighbor, a man I truly loved for his kindness, his wit, and his modest wisdom, made his way over. "Well," he said, "I think your father's intention was to have the earthmover push that sand around before it left but I guess *we* are going to have to do it."

Enthusiastically I began lifting shovels full of sand and throwing them off the top of the mountain. The idea was to evenly distribute the sand within the giant rectangle. Before long I had grown quite weary. I was hot, I was tired, and I could not really see any progress. My respect for my neighbor began to fade as I realized that he had retrieved his lawn chair and lemonade to watch me work.

After seeing me toil for about fifteen minutes, he couldn't stand it any longer. "Come down off of there," he said. "You'll never get the sand moved by beginning at the top. Any sand you move from there you'll have to move several more times."

He explained that I should start at the side of the hill. I should estimate a spot on the hill equal to the height that I wanted all the sand to end up. "Stand upon it," he instructed. "The sand beneath your feet will never have to be moved." So, I picked out a spot about ten percent of the way up the hill. Then, without having to lift the shovel higher than my waist, I dug into the hill, throwing the sand in equal measure to my right and left. Before long, I was standing in the center of a large circle more than twenty feet in diameter. The sand was all exactly at the right height and the original hill was reduced by about a third. I continued to methodically push the sand in circular motions out to the edges of the circle, stepping forward as I did, and the circle continued to expand rapidly in size.

When I completed the job I said to my neighbor, "Wow, I can't believe how easy that was. How did you know that?" He chuckled, "I didn't," he said. "The trick was to step back for a few moments from what at first seemed to be an overwhelming task and think it through. Tasks are always a fraction of the effort if the plan is sound." And then he poured me a glass of lemonade.

Three Poisons in Leadership

Wayne Arnason

In the course of leading Unitarian Universalist congregations and practicing Buddhism, I have realized there are ways in which the "three poisons" that Buddhist teachers warn against reflect common pitfalls for congregational leaders.

The three poisons are greed, anger, and ignorance. Avoiding such nasty things seems like a no-brainer! Here's the problem: the three poisons can be very subtle.

Greed is at play when we want more than we need, or when we soak up a disproportionate amount of resources to accomplish our goals, disadvantaging other areas of need. As church leaders, we can get caught in the trap of greed when our goals are so overblown they are difficult to evaluate, or when we believe that our role or project should command the greatest resources of the staff and budget.

Anger affects our leadership, not so much when we lose our temper, but when we are frustrated by how things unfold beyond our prediction or control. Our frustration may not lead to angry outbursts, but it can prevent us from moving flexibly and adaptively to changing circumstances. Anger in leadership can be described as a reflexive effort to dominate a situation to achieve our desired ends. It reflects an inappropriate use of power. Anger can be at work without anyone raising a voice.

Ignorance happens when as a leader we are vague about our goals, inconsistent in how we communicate about a project's process, or unaware of process and personality issues that can influence the outcomes. There are many leadership education programs and tools available to leaders in Unitarian Universalist congregations. But that doesn't mean that we all use or understand them. With all the new members and leaders continually being welcomed and encouraged in our congregations, it takes discipline and persistence to maintain the leadership culture of a congregation.

What do the three poisons look like? Imagine a new committee chair, recruited to achieve a goal that is so ambitious that it cannot be accomplished in any reasonable time frame. The magnitude of the project encourages the chair to ask for a significant increase in funding for the committee, which puts stress on the rest of the budget. The new chair becomes frustrated by habitual ways of doing work which the longer-term members of the committee think work just fine. He or she tries to exert authority to change these patterns and meets passive resistance, such as people not following through on tasks they didn't really buy into. The minister has failed to tell the chair much about the long-time committee member who has chaired this group twice before. That veteran member is particularly uncomfortable with the changes the new chair wants to make and starts to complain at social occasions about what's happening to this previously strong committee. No one is clear why the new chair is having such a hard time. After eight months the new chair resigns before the church year ends. Sound familiar?

The antidotes to greed, anger, and ignorance are generosity, compassion, and understanding. Generosity implies that ambitious goals are set with the capacity, character, and history of the organization in mind, so that leaders find it easy to feel good about accomplishments achieved. Compassion implies that we do our best to listen to each other and how we believe our gifts and talents are being used to accomplish the goal. If there is a disconnect between the volunteers and the stated goal, we must first listen with an open heart to how that is being experienced before issuing directions or formulating solutions. Understanding implies that we provide our new leaders with the best wisdom about the big picture of our church systems and authority structures. And then implement, examine, and review the process on a regular basis, as succeeding generations of leaders are recruited and fulfill their roles.

Buddhists describe life's challenges as gates through which we can bring our spiritual understandings to everyday life. Generosity, compassion, and understanding take a lifetime to cultivate and nourish and grow. Our leadership roles are among the most important gates we can pass through to make this growth possible.

Leadership

Ned Wight

Walking on eggshells
Waiting for the other shoe to drop
Breathing deeply and counting to fifty
    so you don't say something you'll regret
Anticipating difficulties

Watching for deadly undertow
Getting knocked off your feet by deadly undertow
Swimming like mad to get out of deadly undertow
Standing on the beach wondering how
    you could have overlooked that deadly undertow

Verbal sparring
Wearing one another down
Outlasting the loyal opposition

Staking out the high ground of lofty principles
Fortifying the high ground of lofty principles
Defending the high ground of lofty principles
Obliterating the opposition from the high ground of lofty
    principles

Talking
Talking

Talking
Talking
Talking

Listening
Listening harder
Listening harder to one
Listening harder to one another
Listening harder to one another than you were prepared to

Negotiating differences
Conceding points
Admitting mistakes
Saying "I'm sorry"
Inching toward agreement
Inching toward truth

Reaching agreement
Moving forward
Moving forward together . . .
Walking on eggshells

Wait

Bruce T. Marshall

As leaders, we like to see ourselves as people of action. We encounter a problem and want to fix it—now. But sometimes it doesn't work. Sometimes action doesn't get us anywhere; we just spin our wheels. That's when a better strategy is to wait.

My daughter told of a problem on a take-home physics exam that she just couldn't get. She worked on it for a long time, and it still didn't make sense. So she gave up, went to bed, decided to hand in the exam with that one problem unaddressed.

The next morning, she got up, took a quick look at the stubborn problem and, of course, you know what happened: She saw how to do it. Right away. She could have stayed up all night and never gotten it. But by standing back, waiting, the answer came to her.

We often reach a point when working on a project or approaching a decision when we don't know what to do. At such times, it can be useful to wait. Put the problem on the shelf. Do something else. Take a walk. Give the stars time to align. I have made some bad decisions by taking action before it was time. I do better when I pause for a while to see if a way through this problem presents itself.

The same thing happens in groups. Sometimes we push for a decision before its time. The signs that we're not ready include: uneasiness among several participants, two or more sides that are not hearing each other, irritation at those who take an opposing view, the call to be fearless and decisive no matter the cost. In these moments, it's time to wait. Take a break, move to another topic, tell a joke, table the matter until the next meeting. When you return to the issue, you might find that a shift has occurred. It may not present a final course of action, but a new direction to follow, a new possibility.

You may have heard the advice, "Don't just *do* something, stand there." Sometimes the best course of action is to wait.

Reading for the Standing Committee

Phyllis B. O'Connell

To the Governing Board at the beginning of a new year:

Let us know going into it,

That we will never have all the answers.

We will never get it exactly right.

No matter what we do or how hard we try, we will never please everyone

And we will never finish all the work.

We may never be in complete agreement on anything

And we may hear more criticism than thanks.

Much of what we do will be unseen by most of the congregation.

We will, without even realizing it, reinvent the wheel

And there will be times when we wonder why in the world we signed on for this. But there will be other times too, times when we are able to make real the mission and vision of the church.

There will be times when we laugh together and are grateful to be in this place and be part of the process

Times when our trust builds and our confidence is high and we feel the deep satisfaction of a job well done

Times when we are proud to be counted among the leaders of this congregation.

No policy handbook ever says that what the Standing Committee does is holy work: This is not a committee that leads worship or makes moving music or stirs hearts in prayer. But without your leadership and the work you do, there would be no church.

While no one would ever call serving on the Standing Committee a spiritual discipline, it is, without question, an act of faith.

Everything in Nothing

Sue Phillips

I lost my mind two days into my ministerial internship.

We had a staff retreat at the ministers' house. The office staff was there, our musician, the director of religious education, and the ministers. We spent the day getting to know one another better, sharing personal stories, and planning for the new church year. When it came time to close the retreat, one of the ministers asked me to extinguish the candle, which had been burning quietly all day in a beautiful ceramic chalice. I got up, thinking I would put the candle out with my wet fingers. As I got close to the candle, I realized the flame was much too large and that I would seriously burn my fingers if I put it out like that.

And then it happened. I forgot how to extinguish a candle. I simply could not figure out how to do it. I stood there, completely still, hunched over the flame, for at least five full seconds. Time also stood still, as the staff considered the utter lack of intelligence exhibited by the new intern and the new intern considered the possibility that she had had a stroke. Finally, I said, "How should I do this?" And the minister replied, "Um, you could BLOW it out." So I did.

I was mortified. (And my humiliation did not end that day. The staff gave me grief about it all year—I got a candle snuffer at the staff holiday party.)

I didn't realize at the time that this incident would come to define my experience not only as a minister, but as a spiritual seeker. Forgetting how to blow out that candle was a spiritual lesson. It has to do with becoming a beginner again, with giving up hard-won claims to expertise. It has to do with asking for help, and getting it. It has to do with cultivating what Buddhists call Beginner's Mind.

Beginner's Mind approaches everything as if for the first time. It is the mind that is innocent of preconceptions and expectations, judgments and prejudices. Beginner's Mind is simply present to experience and sees things as they are. Beginner's Mind faces life as a small child, full of curiosity and wonder and amazement. And it is unattached to knowing anything in particular.

Nothingness can be your dear spiritual friend, your greatest spiritual asset. Spiritual wisdom doesn't have to be alchemized. It doesn't come from mysterious ingredients, and it isn't forged in fire. You don't have to try hard to find it: the source of replenishment is already at hand. Beginner's Mind is yours already—all you have to do is nothing at all.

Keep Your Dreams Alive

Hope Johnson

Listen.
Light the way.
Lend a hand.
Make decisions.
Commit.
Take risks.
Fail *forward*.
Build community.
Nurture meaningful relationships.
Be real.
Give thanks.
Invest in someone, or something, that you believe in.
Live.
Love.
Dream.
Dream BIG.
Be transformed.
Change the world.
LEAD.

And keep your dreams alive.

The Rabbis

Dan Hotchkiss

The job was to facilitate what may have been the most diverse and ecumenical gathering of rabbis ever. Tension was apparent even as the rabbis started to arrive: men in black with sidelocks and long beards, women wearing yarmulkes and tallits, spanning all the major branches: Orthodox, Conservative, Reform, and Reconstructionist. One man, unwilling to conform to any of the standard movements, had organized his own. Most amazingly, one rabbi, greeting everyone and vigorously shaking hands with all the men, was from the Lubavitch Chabad, a movement that irritates and worries all the others. Chabad centers, with their mystical ideas and their lack of dues, have become a nuisance, in the view of many synagogues.

With so much variety, you might imagine fifty or a hundred participants, but the little room had only fourteen people in it. Fifteen, if you counted me. Sixteen, if you counted Elaine Goldstein, the woman laying out refreshments, who was about to leave. Elaine worked for the Jewish Federation, where she worried about rabbis. She found them lonely, isolated, stressed, and, for all their Jewish learning, ill-prepared for the realities of life in congregations.

So, one by one, Elaine schmoozed and nudged the rabbis into coming. She called the Alban Institute and got me. My bio on the website says I help with planning, governance, training, conflict, etcetera. Another way to say it, though, is: I walk into a group I don't belong to, where neither I nor anybody else knows what will happen, and I watch while something does.

For this three-day rabbinical retreat, I prepared three days' worth of material. We were going to learn together about growth and decline in congregations, goal-setting and accountability. I might as well have saved myself the trouble.

We started the first evening with a go-around—a check-in— which took much longer than planned, because Elaine was right. These rabbis, even more than many other clergy, had a lot to share, a lot they couldn't talk about with anybody else, because a lot of what a rabbi or a minister experiences, you can't imagine.

Of all the pains and troubles that poured out that evening, one rose right to the top of our agenda. One rabbi, Jacob, had a *yahrzeit*. And he asked the group to form a *minyan* to say *Kaddish*. Minyan is Hebrew for a group of ten who form a quorum for a prayer group. Kaddish is Aramaic for one of the most moving and important prayers in the tradition—the prayer for the dead. Yahrzeit is Yiddish for "year-time," an anniversary. Jacob had lost his brother; he was asking the group to pray with him.

You may realize what rough seas we were heading into: Some of the rabbis wouldn't count a woman in a minyan. Some of them wouldn't even pray unless men were physically separated from the women. And a couple of the women made it clear: They would not be separated, and they would be counted.

I ceased being the facilitator. I became the awed spectator of a learned debate among a group of fourteen rabbis about how to reconcile their differences in order to achieve a goal they all agreed on: Kaddish must be said. A bereaved Jew's request to form a min-yan for his brother was a great *mitzvah*: a non-debatable priority.

This is where we hung for a while. Me, awed at the willingness of people who were in such sharp disagreement about so many things to struggle with their differences in the name of a shared purpose.

At our best, this is what we do in congregations: struggle with our differences in the name of a shared purpose. But we don't, always. Sometimes we lose track of our purpose.

It took most of a day for the rabbis to solve the problem: four-teen of them speaking English, Aramaic, Hebrew, and—when they got really angry—Yiddish.

They all agreed that Kaddish must be said. In that community there was no doubt that covenant had created a new thing: a center of loyalty to which all owed their best and strongest efforts.

In the end, the orthodox conceded the most—they found a local congregation where they could say Kaddish simultaneously with the rabbis' minyan. The women adjusted their participation to accommodate some of the more moderate men. In the end, Jacob had not one minyan but two. And I, a functional illiterate for most of my own retreat, left with a gift of lasting awe for fourteen rabbis' willingness to struggle with their differences in the name of a shared purpose.

A *Prayer for This Gathering*

Laila Ibrahim

Dear God, Spirit of Connection and Creation,

Bless this community, gathered in hope and love for our world, for one another, and for ourselves.

We gather here longing to create a more connected and more just world.

Help us to speak our truth with respect.

Help us to listen with love.

Help us to be patient.

Help us to be forgiving.

Help us to know that here, as in all human endeavors, mistakes are inevitable and perfection is impossible.

And, oh yes, remind us not to take ourselves too seriously.

Amen.

Spiritual Practice in Leadership

Kathleen Rolenz

In a recent conversation with a friend, I mentioned that I couldn't get together with her one night because I was attending a Board of Trustees meeting. Her response was "Oh dear, I'm so sorry." "You don't understand," I said. "Our Board meeting is one of the *best* meetings of the month!"

I was puzzled by her comment, but not surprised. Most folks see Board meetings as a dreadful duty, something that good citizens "should" do, but which entail the high cost of frustration and the feeling that nothing really gets accomplished. Another way to look at it is that meetings of the leadership can be understood as a spiritual practice.

When we engage in a serious spiritual practice, we agree to undertake certain disciplines which are sometimes difficult for fierce individualists and non-conformists to endure. Yet, without discipline, all spiritual practices can become shallow and ultimately not helpful. It would be wise for leaders to develop their own spiritual practices and use them as a way to frame their work as leaders.

For example, in the practice of *lectio divina*—reading scriptures in an intentional way—there are four parts of engagement with text: reading, reflecting, responding and resting. One *reads* a text thoroughly and completely, sometimes from different translations or commentaries; one *reflects* on the text; its meaning both historically and in one's own life; one *responds* to the text from a place of deep listening; and finally, one takes time to *rest* with the text, to see if something new emerges.

Imagine if a group took up the difficult challenge of integrating the spiritual practice of *lectio* with the complex and knotty problems of governance. How might the quality of the conversation change if leaders first read aloud the issue at hand, then reflected in silence for a time on the multiple layers of meaning embedded in the issue, responded (or debated or discussed) from a place of discernment, and finally rested together around the light of the chalice to come to a conclusion?

Acting out of a spiritual practice in times of conflict could change the tenor in the room from confrontation to deeper discernment—an approach more in keeping with our principles as religious people.

Lectio divina is but one example of how a traditional spiritual practice may be incorporated with the work of leadership. Regardless of the form, all spiritual practices share some attributes. They require persistence, patience, and a willingness to practice it. They require submission to a higher authority at times (such as a teacher or laws or, dare I say, by-laws!). They require the discipline of our tongue and restraint of our emotions for the greater good. They require flexibility and adaptability. Most of all, spiritual practices require compassion, both for our imperfect selves and for others, knowing that sometimes, even in our most earnest desire to do good, we fail or are blind to our own agendas that get in the way of good leadership. The old saw that leaders are not born but made is thankfully true. By incorporating spiritual practices we can make ourselves into the kind of leaders whom we ourselves would like to follow.

Meant to Serve

Denise Taft Davidoff

Spirit of life, I know that I am one of the lucky ones. I know that I am meant to serve, gifted with health and skill and spiritual and material wherewithal to do my work in this world.

Help me to make these wilderness days of uncertainty, of yearning, of disequilibrium an experience of learning about myself and others. Renew my appreciation for the precious gift of life and remind me that even when things aren't going my way, they're going my way.

What About That Courage?

Anne Principe

One year, for Palm Sunday, I was asked to craft a message for the Time for All Ages portion of the service. The minister explained that his sermon would explore what called Jesus to Jerusalem. I was to talk with the children about courage, and so I leaned into the task by re-writing a very succinct and powerful definition of courage: "You are not courageous because you aren't afraid. You are courageous when you do something scary or difficult even *when* you're afraid." This quotation is attributed to many.

When we are talking with children—preaching or teaching—we are called into spiritual leadership. In such moments we find ourselves either standing on a fault line or in a sacred circle. No matter how many times I find myself here as a parent and as a religious educator, I'm never really sure what shape, line or circle, I'm standing on. All I can do is responsibly prepare my content and sincerely hone my ability to surrender. What happens after that is what matters most.

And so on that Sunday, I began with no script; I was wired for sound and mobility. Before I got to the story about Jesus and the palms and the last supper and his arrest and his death, I asked aloud,

"Have any of you ever had to do something that was really hard?"

The usual hands go up, but then I see a large hand rise up high. I don't see his face, only his scalp because of his crew cut. He's looking down, possibly writing something. I know some of his story. I know his hand and arm being raised high speaks a powerful truth about the courage he has had to summon in his life.

And while the hands are up, I ask,

"Has anyone ever done anything courageous and you were really, REALLY scared?"

And there is a jag in my throat as more adults raise their hands high, nodding. I am struck by the "all ages" element that I often shoot for and do not always reach.

I see a tiny skinny hand raised proportionally higher than anyone else's. I know this is the hand of a four-year-old, eyes very wide, looking at me. And so I look back and I'm a little scared of why she is so adamant. I walk towards her, nodding, affirming, "And you have had to do something really hard even though it was scary?"

"Yes," she says.

I wonder if she'll be on topic. I hope she'll be appropriate. I worry that people will laugh because she is a child and is cute and is speaking aloud to the congregation.

"Would you like to tell me?" I ask.

"Yes," and she nods and nods, pumping herself up with courage. I wait because it's too late now.

She seems to take a deep breath, nods once more, and says as clear as can be, "I'm learning how to go nigh-nights by myself."

Because I have the microphone, I repeat what she says in affirmation, looking around and collecting the nods of understanding. I practically fall apart because I don't want to move on. I want to sit down on the floor, call a circle, and talk about going nigh-nights all by ourselves. I want to talk about monsters. I want to talk about nightmares. I want to talk about our superpowers. I want to cry. Everyone's eyes—especially the adults—are wide and frozen, and their lids slowly blink in a chorus of, "Yes. Me too."

I'm not sure how the moment ended, but I'm told I wrapped up nicely. I'm told I left them thinking about the courage of Jesus and how he walked forward into a tragic and principled fate.

Deliver Us to Evil

Annette S. Marquis

As a child, I learned to pray the *Our Father*, the Roman Catholic form of *The Lord's Prayer*, which ends not by praising God with "For thine is the kingdom, the power, and the glory, for ever and ever," but rather with the line petitioning God to "deliver us from evil." I stayed awake many nights in my childhood bed imagining the evil God might deliver me from. My image of God was of a force field that, if I were good enough, would surround me and keep me protected from evil in the world. I prayed I would be good enough.

As I grew older, I realized I could no longer ask God to deliver me from evil. I couldn't hide from it, safe behind a protective shield, and expect evil to dissipate on its own—I had to play an active role in dispelling evil in whatever ways I could. I came to understand that it is in the absence of love that evil propagates, and, in the presence of love that evil dissipates.

So instead of praying to God to deliver me from evil, I began praying for the Spirit of Life to deliver me *to* evil, to give me the courage to go where evil exists and supplant it with love. As a Unitarian Universalist, I learned how to make my voice heard by joining with others to stand against injustice and hatred. For, like first responders in a disaster, it is only when we run toward evil and overpower it with love that we interrupt the forces that have allowed evil to prosper, and in so doing, move the world a step closer to heaven.

So now, instead of the prayer I was taught as a child, I pray these words:

Spirit of Life, which exists wherever there is love,
Blessed be all Your Names.
Strengthen our will
To create heaven on earth,
And help us embody a peace-filled world.
Give us all our daily bread.
Teach us to forgive ourselves for our failings,
And to forgive those who have failed us.
Deliver us to evil
And give us the courage to transform it with Love.
For Love is the power, and the glory,
For ever and ever.
Amen.

As If God Were There

Terry Sweetser

I was seven years old when I had my first encounter with theology. My mother made a batch of fudge, put it in the fridge, and decreed it could not be touched until after supper. I was not pleased. I conjured every scheme I could to sneak some, but someone was always lurking in the kitchen.

About four in the afternoon, I got an incredible break. My mother and sister had to head out for the store, leaving me alone. Mom must have been reading my mind because she gave me a warning on the way out: "Just because I'm not here, don't think you are alone with the fudge. God is watching you!"

The word *theology* means God-study. After they drove off I studied hard. It did not take long for me to conclude I was a seven-year-old atheist. That fudge tasted good!

Unfortunately for me, Mom had counted the pieces, and the re-count on her return showed a deficit of three. When asked how I had dared to steal fudge right in front of God, I said, "I don't believe in God." My ever practical Unitarian Universalist mother swatted my butt and sent me to my room saying, "It would be in your best interests to act as if God were there!"

The personal God who could legislate justice and control the universe died for me that day, but a passionate interest in what people mean by the idea of God was born. I sense it is a passion most of us share. Unitarian Universalists really get worked up about God.

For all practical purposes though, Mom was right: It's in our best interests to act as if God were there.

Tolerance for Repetition

William G. Sinkford

We hold a vision of the beloved community. Our mission describes what we are called to do to move toward that vision. Our covenant consists of the promises we make to one another about how we will walk together as we live out our mission.

Many of us have been in gatherings where we craft vision, mission, and covenant statements. There is always plenty of butcher paper taped to the walls; we brainstorm the elements of these foundational understandings; a facilitator asks questions when clarity is hard to come by and then faithfully records the statements. At some point, the "magic dots" come out, the suggestions are prioritized and . . . with a little wordsmithing . . . *voila!* The congregation or organization has its statements.

The statements are circulated by email, posted on the website and, all too often, rarely referred to again. One of the leaders' most important roles is to remind the community of these commitments. Not occasionally, and not only during times of stress, but again and again. Leaders need to help the community embody its central aspirations. It is a religious practice and a discipline to take those aspirations seriously.

In that process, the vision, mission, and covenant statements become more than simply well-intentioned documents, but living parts of our life in community. They inform our responses to particular challenges. They develop meaning that grows out of their use. Often our understanding of them changes and grows in a dialogical process of action and reflection.

Tolerance for repetition is rarely cited when listing leadership qualities. But good leaders not only tolerate repetition, they endorse it as a central tool to help congregations and organizations stay centered and faithful.

The Mosaic Makers

Alicia Forde

You are Mosaic Makers, practitioners of justice,
called to respond to brokenness in the world,
restoring beauty by joining in solidarity
with the least of these,
the poor, the undocumented, the wrongly persecuted
because of sex or gender identity or race.

You, Mosaic Makers, practitioners of justice,
will minister to each other
for this ministry needs your energy, your passion,
your hands in order to thrive.
It needs your wildly beating heart to animate its spirit.

Being Mosaic Makers isn't easy,
the pieces can be so tiny.
It's difficult to see the whole picture,
you always risk making a mistake and needing to undo.
You will have moments of dis-ease, of needing to apologize.
Make amends, restore your covenant.
You will have moments of fatigue.
Share leadership, invite others
to share this vision and co-create with you.

You, Mosaic Makers, practitioners of justice,
your work is act of gratitude for those who came before
and for that which is yet to be . . .

How blessed you are. How blessed we are to be in this together.

How Will You Use Your Gifts?

Don Southworth

One of the first things I saw on my first day of seminary at Starr King School for the Ministry in August 1996 was the official school T-shirt. On the front of the shirt was a beautiful drawing of a sand dollar. I discovered the importance and meaning of the sand dollar later that morning during our opening worship service. Rebecca Parker, the president of Starr King, spoke poetically and movingly about the sand dollar's history at the school and its symbolism for our time there. For decades incoming students have been given a sand dollar as a welcome gift in a ritual to honor the gifts we brought to the school and to represent the grace and mystery of our vocations to ministry. We were each invited to choose a sand dollar to take with us on our journeys.

With tears in my eyes, I prayerfully selected the sand dollar that I knew would be the perfect companion on my road to ministry. When I returned to my seat, and as I lovingly fondled it, my precious sand dollar shattered into several pieces and soon was nothing but sand dollar dust. I realized that this probably wasn't a good omen for my future, so I snuck back to the basket to take another. Certain that nobody saw me, I slunk back to my seat and gently placed the new sand dollar in my pocket. Fifteen minutes later, when I went to touch my sacred sand dollar, I discovered it too was in pieces. Convinced that the Gods were telling me something about my choice to pursue the ministry, I quietly dumped my sand dollar dust into the garbage and wondered if seminary was the right place for me.

Fortunately, the T-shirt on the wall had writing on the back as well. It said: "How will you use your gifts?" Since sand dollars did not seem to be my thing, I hoped I could do a better job with that question. On that day, that question became one of the guiding lights of my life and ministry. How will you use your gifts? I have been blessed to be surrounded by faculty, friends, family, colleagues, and congregations committed to living that question with me. It is a question with the power to transform the world.

How will you use your gifts? Imagine what would happen if every one of us committed to fully living out the answer to that question and helping others to do the same. Imagine if every person in the world overcame their doubts, fears, and oppressions and shared all their gifts.

We have the power to change and heal the world when we use our gifts to bless the world. And what better place to practice than in our religious communities, where we are encouraged to bring our unique talents, skills, passions, and dreams, and share them as widely as we can — even on those days when we feel as imperfect as a broken sand dollar.

You and I are miracles, my friends. We are packages of gifts that have never been seen before in the history of the world and will never be seen again. Our potential, our greatness, lie in how well we open our packages, our lives, and share them with other people. To paraphrase the words of Dr. Martin Luther King Jr.: Everybody can be great. Because everybody can share their gifts with the world. You don't need a master of divinity degree to share your gifts. You don't have to make your subject and verb agree to share your gifts with the world. You only need a heart full of grace. A soul generated by love. (And maybe a pocket full of sand dollar dust!)

Theology of Accompaniment

Janice Marie Johnson

I got an important glimpse into the spiritual practice of being in partnership when I learned about the theology of accompaniment. The term comes from Cuban-American theologian Roberto Goizueta in his book *Caminemos con Jesus*. Rev. Jackie Clements introduced me and many others to the concept in New Orleans at "Finding Our Way Home," an annual gathering of Unitarian Universalist religious professionals of color.

Clements described how the verb *acompañar* in Spanish differs in complexity, texture, and weight from the English *to accompany*, which can be used for something as mundane to going to the grocery store with someone. The Spanish word connotes something deeper. "It's like being joined at the hip," said a colleague at the retreat.

In a review of Goizueta's work, professor and chaplain Fr. Kurt Messick notes that a theology of accompaniment "has many implications, including a recognition of the value of human beings regardless of gender . . . as well as a recognition of the importance of theological themes all through life: in the home, in the workplace, in the social arena. It is our task, regardless of our starting point, to walk with, or accompany, these people. To walk with the poor does not simply mean a geographic relocation. It means becoming intensely aware of their conditions—body, mind, spirit, hope, future—and how these things differ from mainstream Western culture. It is also a call to the development of interior life, as a means of strengthening the identity of those from whom culture often robs or ignores."

When I think of partnership, I think of striving to empower the community and building bridges. I think of working collaboratively with various organizations and individuals—especially those who understand the profound difference between providing services to the disenfranchised and breaking bread with siblings.

A theology of accompaniment calls us to move beyond "othering," beyond tolerating, beyond embracing. It calls us to honor our siblings as the unique and precious beings that we all are—in spite of class, race, ethnicity, ability, and all else that would divide us.

Accompaniment is a choice. One that can resonate profoundly as a spiritual practice of being in partnership.

Transformational Leadership

Meg Riley

When did you first experience powerful, love-creating leadership? Who bent you toward love at an early age, and how?

When I look back on all the paths I walked as a child, the person who lights up most clearly is Mrs. Graham, my third grade teacher in Overbrook School in Charleston, West Virginia. Mrs. Graham loved us. She loved kids. She loved me. She thought we were funny, and interesting—that *I* was funny and interesting. She listened to us. To me!

And she told us stories about herself. She told us who she was. She loved woodpeckers, and so our classroom rows were named after them. "Okay, the pileated may line up first for lunch. . . ." I have loved woodpeckers ever since, with a bit of her heart as well as my own.

On the day that John F. Kennedy was shot, Mrs. Graham was standing at the front of Room 3. Randall Hainey's mom came running in the back door with a transistor radio to tell us. Mrs. Graham handed out lined paper and said solemnly, "You will remember this day always. Write down exactly what happened, because you'll want to tell your grandchildren about it. You are part of history."

I remember sitting there in disbelief. Someone could shoot the president? I was part of history? Mrs. Hainey and her transistor radio would matter to my grandchildren? I might have grandchildren? Mrs. Graham believed in us, not just as children, but as life itself, as part of the living movement of history.

Transformational leaders recognize people's worth and value, even before they can see it themselves. Transformational leaders see patterns that value every person's place in history. Transformational leaders know, in the words of rapper Lupe Fiasco, If you don't become an actor, you'll never be a factor. Transformational leaders create actors wherever they go.

Facing Fear, Trusting Love

Manish Mishra-Marzetti

Every day, as leaders within a spiritual community, we must realize that our actions and inactions affect dozens if not hundreds of lives. How do we prioritize the list of pressing needs? What do we have time to get to today? What will have to wait yet another day before the needed time emerges?

Will those decisions mean that someone who needs care and support might not receive it today? Will we meet our fundraising and budgetary goals, or fall short? Will someone leave our Sunday service feeling less welcome than they should? Will we have enough volunteers for our religious education classes?

The possibility of failure abounds.

We are engaged in a fallible, human enterprise, but it is one that simultaneously transcends our finitude. Amid the uncertainty, amid the risk of failure, can we remember why we stepped forward?

To make a difference in someone's life.

To help build and create healthy community.

To share our gifts and talents with the world around us.

To be the best we can be, and bring out the best in others.

Grounded in these intentions, it's never possible to fail. The world needs every bit of good that each of us has to offer. Do what you can. Trust that gifts offered in love will be received in the spirit of love. Trust that what we are contributing to is far greater than any one of us. Trust that even when we fall short, the good that we are able to do matters. Greatly.

Get in the Game (Show)!

Vanessa Rush Southern

Do you remember Let's Make a Deal? There was Monty Hall, the convivial host who invited contestants to pick prizes behind doors. And do you remember how the contestants had to be dressed in costumes? And how they would clamor for attention, each more absurd than the next?

When I was little, we lived in Los Angeles and my mother was given a ticket to Let's Make a Deal. Actually, it was a ticket that allowed you to go to the studio lot and stand outside in a crowd to maybe get chosen to be inside the studio for the shooting of the show. My mom is not a flamboyant character, but she rose to the occasion. She put on all my dad's fishing equipment—thigh-high waders, a flannel shirt, a fishing vest festooned with lures, one of those silly fisherman hats, and a fishing net and pole. Then she went to the studio and stood outside with all the other dressed-up fools and waited until the studio man came out and walked from one end of the line to the other, picking people to be on the show.

As he approached, my mother tried to be perky and "choose-able" (whatever that means) and this man walked right by her, picking people out of the line before her and after her. My mom realized what was happening, and that if she didn't do something she wouldn't get chosen—and would have taken a day off from work, dressed in a ridiculous outfit, for nothing. She did something unprecedented for her. In a moment of whimsy and gumption, she threw her fishing net over the studio exec's head. He turned around, only slightly amused, and said, "Okay, lady, you're in."

That was it.

Inside the studio, Mom did her best to wave her hands and jump up and down to be chosen to actually compete. She even coined her own catch phrase: "I'm fishing for a deal!" We have black and white photographs taken of the television screen (this was before VCRs). She wasn't chosen, but she got in and had a good time.

I remember this episode because, like my mom, we sometimes go into life a little underprepared and misled. We have our ticket to play, but we don't know if we'll get in the game. We can stand out-side and say we were there—at the courthouse steps, on the company payroll, in the pews on Sunday—but what it takes to get in on the real action is risk, and a willingness to be outside our comfort zone.

None of us knows what we are doing when we show up in new places. And the ways in are never clear. Still, you ask to meet with the senator so she can hear what you think because the courthouse steps are a little far from her office. You send a proposal to the HR director because you think the policy about family leave creates less goodwill than it might. You make an appointment to see the minis-ter because you have these gifts and you want to use them in service of the mission you love. All of a sudden, you are on the radar. Inside the studio. Fishers of men and women. Servants of the good.

Sometimes you just have to leap in, dress up, stretch out a hand, cast a net, and see what happens. It may not work. Or it may get us halfway to where we wanted to be or achieve half the results we'd dreamed, but that's closer than the parking lot. And with enough of us risking, some of us are bound to get in. And the rest of us can swap stories about the fun we had trying.

We Covenant

Janice Marie Johnson

Covenants are intentional.
Covenants are audacious.
Covenants are a promise
that can change our lives together in this faith.

Together, we will be stronger.
Together, we will be wiser.
Together, we will be gentler.

We promise
to recognize our uniqueness
to treasure our faith
to honor our neighbors with holiness.

We covenant to be committed to each other
to consider each as significant
to consider each as valuable.

We covenant
to be invitational
to be accepting
to speak grace-filled truth
to forgive each other
over and over again.

And, yes,
to love.

Our Covenant stands firm.
It is our embodiment of faith in each other.
It is our blessing of each other.
It is our commitment to each other.

May we hold this community as a precious gift.
May we hold our relationships as gifts that transcend borders.

May we carry forth
the intention of our Covenant
the audacity of our Covenant
the promise of our Covenant
now and in the years to come.

May it be so.

We Are the People Who Choose

Jane Ranney Rzepka

So I'm in Istanbul, in the marketplace, adrift in the covered bazaar and, insanely, I'm trying to blend in. I'm amidst tables of figs, flip flops, saffron, carpets, apple tea, and hookahs. I'm walking past booth after booth of pistachios, evil eyes, satellite dishes, Islamic holy books, Bart Simpson T-shirts, brass trays, and harem girl outfits.

Harem girl outfits. And the fellow in the harem outfit booth looks at me for a split second and says in perfect English: "It is your destiny."

This particular sales pitch did not work. At least to date, I have not put my name on the harem girl sign-up sheet, regardless of my destiny. I laughed out loud and there, in the Turkish covered bazaar, experienced a moment of perfect clarity: I am a Unitarian Universalist, and we are people who choose.

And that, my friends, is the point.

You are choosing your religion, and what you're going to believe about god, and good and evil, and justice, and what you think they mean. You are choosing how you handle death, how you're going to change the world, how you're going to connect with the cosmos, and how you're going to get through the day. It's your religion, and your church.

It's your church, and maybe you like rocking babies in the Nursery, or you like designing shelves, or you'd just like to try; you're a natural-born leader or you'd like to test your wings at chairing a committee. You're a bit of a ham, or terrified of public speaking, either way it's your church, your vision, it's all within your power. You are choosing your faith.

Whether you are chatty or mute, analytical or artistic, you with your personal finances bar graphed on your computer, you who feel at home in the kitchen, you who have a wealth of intuition, you whose watch beeps on the hour, you who wonder what day it is, you whose socks don't match, you are welcome here because, after all, this is your church and you know this is good stuff.

You know what you want from church. You've made your decisions, you know what counts in your life, you know what you like. Why else would you fill out a pledge card, guilt free and happily? You have your own reasons to celebrate.

You know where you are headed. And whether you're looking for peace and harmony, or wholeness, or a more just world, you've arrived. And whether you want to teach the children a sense of their inherent worth, or that their faith and lives are one, or a love for the adventures of life, you're here together. You've arrived. And whether you're looking for a community of love, or a sense of transcendence, healing or comfort, here you are together. You've arrived.

Letter to the People of the Future

John Cummins

My Distant Children:

You will look back on us with astonishment at the truths that stared us in the face, and which we did not see. You will look with wonder at the bright toys we created, and used only for the rape of the planet, and one another.

It will seem strange beyond believing that we reached for the stars, and did not know the simplest principles of living well together.

But know this also, you of the future, you with your libraries and fountains, you in your star cities. Know that even in our slumbers, we dreamed. In our fumbling, shadowed search for mistaken glories, even in our clumsy cruelties, it was for you that we dreamed!

Beneath the piled-up centuries, below the lost and ruined rubble of all our striving, it was you who lay safe, enfolded in the womb of our dreaming. You, the first cause of all our daring! Even now, it brings comfort to know that it shall one day be as the wise among us have foretold.

In that far age, in the chrysalis of time, it will be your source of pride that your ancestors, born into a universe without justice or mercy, bethought themselves of justice and mercy, and put them there!

Remember us for this.

A *Blessing for Those Who Minister*

Elea Kemler

Blessed are those who minister.

Blessed are those who welcome the quirky, the lost, and the unwanted, the ones whose sweetness usually goes unseen.

Blessed are those who treat the fearful with gentleness and can see the face of the child in the one who is unkind.

Blessed are those who do not use sarcasm as a weapon when their feelings are hurt and who tell hard truths with the intent to heal and not to wound.

Blessed are those who hold in their keeping whole books of stories that can never be told, stories of betrayal and shame and sorrow, stories of how life shatters into pieces like glass.

Blessed are those who offer comfort and hope in the face of the wreckage, who show up as soon as the news goes out, who meet the police on the doorstep, who hold out their hands.

Blessed are those who sit with the upwelling of grief and the aching emptiness, who do not flinch back from pain, especially when it is raw and angry and new.

Blessed are those who dare to find words to speak of such fleet, shimmering things as hope and grace and who know to speak of faith quietly and mostly in poems.

Blessed are those who hold such stillness in their spirits that it radiates outward for others to rest in.

Blessed are those who minister.